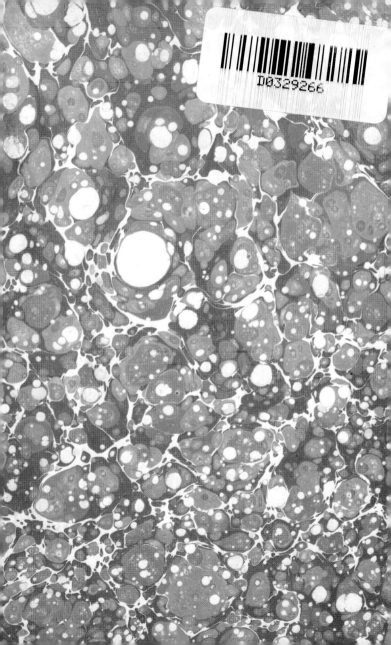

GREAT ENGLISH POETS

GREAT ENGLISH POETS

Elizabeth
Barrett Browning

Edited and with an introduction
by Peter Porter

 Clarkson N. Potter, Inc./Publishers NEW YORK

Published in the United States by Clarkson N. Potter, Inc.,
201 East 50th Street, New York, New York 10022
and distributed by Crown Publishers, Inc.
Published in Great Britain by Aurum Press Ltd.,
10 Museum Street, London WC1A 1JS

CLARKSON N. POTTER, POTTER, THE GREAT POETS
and colophon are trademarks of Clarkson N. Potter Inc.

Picture research by Juliet Brightmore

Manufactured in Hong Kong

Library of Congress Cataloging-in-Publication Data

Browning, Elizabeth Barrett, 1806–1861.
[Poems. Selections]
Elizabeth Barrett Browning/edited and
with an introduction by Peter Porter.
p. cm. – (Great English poets)
ISBN 0-517-58935-4 :$10.00
I. Porter. Peter. II. Title. III. Series.
PR4182.P67   1992
821'.8 - dc20   91-40456
CIP
10 9 8 7 6 5 4 3 2 1
First Edition

CONTENTS

INTRODUCTION

Literature abounds in reputations that continue unfaded though the works which made them are no longer current. Such would be the case with Byron if his letters, a handful of lyrics and *Don Juan* were not still admired. Life has replaced art; the biography excites us while much of the poetry is ignored. Elizabeth Barrett Browning is an unhappy example of public familiarity hardly going beyond her name, other than a few half-remembered romantic details of her elopement, exile and early death. There is a second reason for this effacement – she married one of the greatest poets in the English language, Robert Browning. When they first met, she was the lionized author, one of the most celebrated poets of the early Victorian period. He was a young and unread beginner. At the time of her death in 1861 she was still the better-known of the two. Robert lived on until 1889 and became, after Tennyson, the premier poet of the century. Today he is an immortal, the Father of Modernism, while Elizabeth Barrett's poetry is largely unpublished and unread.

Yet her fame is potent enough in two directions – in romantic legend and through feminism. The first was given currency in a play of the 1930s which became one of the box-office hits of all time – Rudolf Besier's *The Barretts of Wimpole Street*. Here the story of the robust Robert's wooing of the valetudinarian Elizabeth was turned into a triumph of love over parental opposition. The reality was very different, of course, but the legend has sufficient truth in it to make Elizabeth's deliverance from her Wimpole Street sickbed, to begin a new and vigorous existence in Tuscany, a true-life romance. What the play could only hint at was Elizabeth's commanding intelligence, and the originality of her mind. She read Greek and Latin, was absorbed in politics and had an understanding of the social system of her day unique among English women poets. At the same time, her championing of Italian independence (see *Casa Guidi Windows*) was as practical as it was generous.

Feminism has esteemed Elizabeth largely for extra-literary reasons. Her long verse narrative *Aurora Leigh* is undoubtedly a feminist tract, but like all original writers Elizabeth could see more than one side of any case, and this remarkable tale of a woman poet championing a working-class girl who is wronged by an upper-class lover is ironic in its presentation of the need for female liberation. But her scorn for masculine patronage is real: 'How arrogant men are! Even philanthropists/ Who try to take a wife up in the way/ They put down a subscription cheque.' What fits in less well with feminism is her piety, her deep-seated familiarity with the Bible, the works of the Fathers and the early Christian poets. 'God' is probably the most frequently encountered word in her poetry.

Elizabeth Barrett was a copious poet. She even produced an imitation epic *The Battle of Marathon* before she was fifteen. Throughout her life her models were the Greek and Latin classics and the English poets of the Jacobean age and the eighteenth century. Each of her poems is a well-made artefact, and, it must be admitted, many show signs of her laborious craftsmanship. The originality of her vision develops as she faces the reality of the Victorian world she was able to observe from her privileged position. She does not exhibit those touches we can call 'feminine', as Christina Rossetti and, to a far greater extent, Emily Dickinson do. She can strike with great force: nobody summed up the shock of Napoleon as potently as she did in one line in her poem 'Crowned and Buried' – 'And kings crept out again to feel the sun'. Her lyrics are often finely honed and delightfully light – namely 'The Sea-Mew' and 'The Lady's Yes'. Nevertheless, she is usually serious and often sententious, but always liberal of attitude and wonderfully free of vanity. In *Aurora Leigh* she writes, 'For me, I wrote/ False poems, like the rest, and thought them true/ Because myself was true in writing them.' Her diction is unexpectedly modern – she uses words such as 'teens', 'archetype' and 'inflatus' without embarrassment.

Elizabeth was the eldest child of Edward Moulton Barrett, whose wealth derived originally from plantations in Jamaica. She was born in 1806 in the North of England and became the famous invalid of Wimpole Street only after serious illness in early womanhood. Her Tuscan life with Robert Browning was largely happy, despite poor health complicated by miscarriages, but the Italian heat and the rigours of travelling to England and throughout the Continent wore her out. After her death, Robert Browning never again visited Florence and testified, in poem after poem, to his devotion to her memory and to the fierce intellectual spirit which had inhabited so slight and sickly a frame.

Because her finest poems tend to be overlong, I have made several radical shortenings in producing this selection without, I believe, damaging the works concerned; but a full account of my editing in each case is given on page 60. The following pages offer an essence of an unfairly neglected poet whose nature was as realistic as it was passionate. As she wrote in *Sonnets from the Portuguese*, 'God's gifts put man's best dreams to shame.' Her own gifts deserve to be more plainly on view.

From
SONNETS FROM THE PORTUGUESE

Suite of Sonnets

Unlike are we, unlike, O princely Heart!
Unlike our uses and our destinies.
Our ministering two angels look surprise
On one another, as they strike athwart
Their wings in passing. Thou, bethink thee, art
A guest for queens to social pageantries,
With gages from a hundred brighter eyes
Than tears even can make mine, to play thy part
Of chief musician. What hast *thou* to do
With looking from the lattice-lights at me,
A poor, tired, wandering singer, . . . singing
    through
The dark, and leaning up a cypress tree?
The chrism is on thine head, – on mine, the dew, –
And Death must dig the level where these agree.

Thou hast thy calling to some palace-floor,
Most gracious singer of high poems! where
The dancers will break footing, from the care
Of watching up thy pregnant lips for more.
And dost thou lift this house's latch too poor
For hand of thine? and canst thou think and bear
To let thy music drop here unaware
In folds of golden fulness at my door?
Look up and see the casement broken in,
The bats and owlets builders in the roof!
My cricket chirps against thy mandolin.
Hush, call no echo up in further proof
Of desolation! there's a voice within
That weeps . . . as thou must sing . . . alone, aloof.

I lift my heavy heart up solemnly,
As once Electra her sepulchral urn,
And, looking in thine eyes, I overturn
The ashes at thy feet. Behold and see
What a great heap of grief lay hid in me,
And how the red wild sparkles dimly burn
Through the ashen greyness. If thy foot in scorn

Could tread them out to darkness utterly,
It might be well perhaps. But if instead
Thou wait beside me for the wind to blow
The grey dust up, . . . those laurels on thine head,
O my Belovèd, will not shield thee so,
That none of all the fires shall scorch and shred
The hair beneath. Stand further off then! go.

Yet, love, mere love, is beautiful indeed
And worthy of acceptation. Fire is bright,
Let temple burn, or flax. An equal light
Leaps in the flame from cedar-plank or weed.
And love is fire. And when I say at need
I love thee . . . mark! . . . *I love thee* – in thy sight
I stand transfigured, glorified aright,
With conscience of the new rays that proceed
Out of my face toward thine. There's nothing low
In love, when love the lowest: meanest creatures
Who love God, God accepts while loving so.
And what I *feel*, across the inferior features
Of what I *am*, doth flash itself, and show
How that great work of Love enhances Nature's.

And wilt thou have me fashion into speech
The love I bear thee, finding words enough,
And hold the torch out, while the winds are rough
Between our faces, to cast light on each? –
I drop it at thy feet. I cannot teach
My hand to hold my spirit so far off
From myself . . . me . . . that I should bring thee
        proof
In words, of love hid in me out of reach.
Nay, let the silence of my womanhood
Commend my woman-love to thy belief, –
Seeing that I stand unwon, however wooed,
And rend the garment of my life, in brief,
By a most dauntless, voiceless fortitude,
Lest one touch of this heart convey its grief.

If thou must love me, let it be for nought
Except for love's sake only. Do not say
'I love her for her smile . . . her look . . . her way
Of speaking gently, . . . for a trick of thought
That falls in well with mine, and certes brought
A sense of pleasant ease on such a day' –
For these things in themselves, Belovèd, may
Be changed, or change for thee, – and love, so
        wrought

May be unwrought so. Neither love me for
Thine own dear pity's wiping my cheeks dry, –
A creature might forget to weep, who bore
Thy comfort long, and lose thy love thereby!
But love me for love's sake, that evermore
Thou may'st love on, through love's eternity.

Say over again, and yet once over again,
That thou dost love me. Though the word repeated
Should seem 'a cuckoo-song,' as thou dost treat it,
Remember, never to the hill or plain,
Valley and wood, without her cuckoo-strain
Comes the fresh Spring in all her green completed.
Belovèd, I, amid the darkness greeted
By a doubtful spirit-voice, in that doubt's pain
Cry, . . . 'Speak once more . . . thou lovest!' Who
        can fear
Too many stars, though each in heaven shall roll, –
Too many flowers, though each shall crown the
        year?
Say thou dost love me, love me, love me – toll
The silver iterance! – only minding, Dear,
To love me also in silence with thy soul.

I lived with visions for my company
Instead of men and women, years ago,
And found them gentle mates, nor thought to know
A sweeter music than they played to me.
But soon their trailing purple was not free
Of this world's dust, – their lutes did silent grow,
And I myself grew faint and blind below
Their vanishing eyes. Then THOU didst come . . . to be,
Belovèd, what they seemed. Their shining fronts,
Their songs, their splendours (better, yet the same,
As river-water hallowed into fonts),
Met in thee, and from out thee overcame
My soul with satisfaction of all wants –
Because God's gifts put man's best dreams to shame.

My letters! all dead paper, . . . mute and white!
And yet they seem alive and quivering
Against my tremulous hands which loose the string
And let them drop down on my knee to-night.
This said, . . . he wished to have me in his sight
Once, as a friend: this fixed a day in spring
To come and touch my hand . . . a simple thing,
Yet I wept for it! – this, . . . the paper's light . . .
Said, *Dear I love thee*; and I sank and quailed
As if God's future thundered on my past.
This said, *I am thine* – and so its ink has paled
With lying at my heart that beat too fast.
And this . . . O Love, thy words have ill availed
If, what this said, I dared repeat at last!

First time he kissed me, he but only kissed
The fingers of this hand wherewith I write;
And ever since, it grew more clean and white,
Slow to world-greetings, quick with its 'Oh, list,'
When the angels speak. A ring of amethyst
I could not wear here, plainer to my sight,
Than that first kiss. The second passed in height
The first, and sought the forehead, and half missed,

Half falling on the hair. O beyond meed!
That was the chrism of love, which love's own
       crown
With sanctifying sweetness, did precede.
The third upon my lips was folded down
In perfect, purple state; since when, indeed,
I have been proud and said, 'My love, my own.'

I thank all who have loved me in their hearts,
With thanks and love from mine. Deep thanks to all
Who paused a little near the prison-wall
To hear my music in its louder parts
Ere they went onward, each one to the mart's
Or temple's occupation, beyond call.
But thou, who, in my voice's sink and fall
When the sob took it, thy divinest Art's
Own instrument didst drop down at thy foot
To harken what I said between my tears, . . .
Instruct me how to thank thee! – Oh, to shoot
My soul's full meaning into future years,
That *they* should lend it utterance, and salute
Love that endures, from Life that disappears!

How do I love thee? Let me count the ways.
I love thee to the depth and breadth and height
My soul can reach, when feeling out of sight
For the ends of Being and ideal Grace.
I love thee to the level of everyday's
Most quiet need, by sun and candelight.
I love thee freely, as men strive for Right;
I love thee purely, as they turn from Praise.
I love thee with the passion put to use
In my old griefs, and with my childhood's faith.
I love thee with a love I seemed to lose
With my lost saints, – I love thee with the breath,
Smiles, tears, of all my life! – and, if God choose,
I shall but love thee better after death.

Song

Weep, as if you thought of laughter!
Smile, as tears were coming after!
Marry your pleasures to your woes;
And think life's green well worth its rose!

No sorrow will your heart betide,
Without a comfort by its side;
The sun may sleep in his sea-bed,
But you have starlight overhead.

Trust not to Joy! the rose of June,
When opened wide, will wither soon;
Italian days without twilight
Will turn them suddenly to night.

Joy, most changeful of all things,
Flits away on rainbow wings;
And when they look the gayest, know,
It is that they are spread to go!

The Lady's Yes

'Yes,' I answered you last night;
 'No,' this morning, sir, I say.
Colours seen by candle-light
 Will not look the same by day.

When the viols played their best,
 Lamps above and laughs below,
Love me sounded like a jest,
 Fit for *yes* or fit for *no*.

Call me false or call me free,
 Vow, whatever light may shine –
No man on your face shall see
 Any grief for change on mine.

Yet the sin is on us both;
 Time to dance is not to woo;
Wooing light makes fickle troth,
 Scorn of *me* recoils on *you*.

Learn to win a lady's faith
 Nobly, as the thing is high,
Bravely, as for life and death,
 With a loyal gravity.

Lead her from the festive boards,
  Point her to the starry skies;
Guard her, by your truthful words,
  Pure from courtship's flatteries.

By your truth she shall be true,
  Ever true, as wives of yore;
And her *yes*, once said to you,
  SHALL be Yes for evermore.

The Sea-Mew

How joyously the young sea-mew
Lay dreaming on the waters blue
Whereon our little bark had thrown
A little shade, the only one,
But shadows ever man pursue.

Familiar with the waves and free
As if their own white foam were he,
His heart upon the heart of ocean
Lay learning all its mystic motion,
And throbbing to the throbbing sea.

And such a brightness in his eye
As if the ocean and the sky
Within him had lit up and nurst
A soul God gave him not at first,
To comprehend their majesty.

We were not cruel, yet did sunder
His white wing from the blue waves under,
And bound it, while his fearless eyes
Shone up to ours in calm surprise,
As deeming us some ocean wonder.

We bore our ocean bird unto
A grassy place where he might view
The flowers that curtsey to the bees,
The waving of the tall green trees,
The falling of the silver dew.

But flowers of earth were pale to him
Who had seen the rainbow fishes swim;
And when earth's dew around him lay
He thought of ocean's wingèd spray,
And his eye waxed sad and dim.

The green trees round him only made
A prison with their darksome shade;
And drooped his wing, and mournèd he
For his own boundless glittering sea –
Albeit he knew not they could fade.

Then One her gladsome face did bring,
Her gentle voice's murmuring,
In ocean's stead his heart to move
And teach him what was human love:
He thought it a strange mournful thing.

He lay down in his grief to die,
(First looking to the sea-like sky
That hath no waves) because, alas!
Our human touch did on him pass,
And with our touch, our agony.

THE CRY OF THE HUMAN

The plague runs festering through the town,
    And never a bell is tolling,
And corpses, jostled 'neath the moon,
    Nod to the dead-cart's rolling.
The young child calleth for the cup,
    The strong man brings it weeping;
The mother from her babe looks up,
    And shrieks away its sleeping.
                                        Be pitiful, O God!

The plague of gold strikes far and near,
    And deep and strong it enters;
This purple chimar which we wear
    Makes madder than the centaur's:
Our thoughts grow blank, our words grow strange,
    We cheer the pale gold-diggers –
Each soul is worth so much on 'Change,
    And marked, like sheep, with figures.
                                        Be pitiful, O God!

The curse of gold upon the land
    The lack of bread enforces;
The rail-cars snort from strand to strand,
    Like more of Death's white horses!

The rich preach 'rights' and 'future days',
  And hear no angel scoffing, –
The poor die mute – with starving gaze
  On corn-ships in the offing.

                        Be pitiful, O God!

We meet together at the feast,
  To private mirth betake us;
We stare down in the winecup, lest
  Some vacant chair should shake us.
We name delight and pledge it round –
  'It shall be ours to-morrow!'
God's seraphs, do your voices sound
  As sad in naming sorrow?

                        Be pitiful, O God!

The happy children come to us,
  And look up in our faces:
They ask us – 'Was it thus, and thus,
  When we were in their places?' –
We cannot speak; – we see anew
  The hills we used to live in,
And feel our mother's smile press through
  The kisses she is giving.

                        Be pitiful, O God!

We sit on hills our childhood wist,
   Woods, hamlets, streams, beholding:
The sun strikes through the farthest mist,
   The city's spire to golden.
The city's golden spire it was,
   When hope and health were strongest,
But now it is the churchyard grass
   We look upon the longest.
                    Be pitiful, O God!

From
THE CRY OF THE CHILDREN

Do ye hear the children weeping, O my brothers,
    Ere the sorrow comes with years?
They are leaning their young heads against their
    mothers,
        And *that* cannot stop their tears.
The young lambs are bleating in the meadows,
    The young birds are chirping in the nest,
The young fawns are playing with the shadows,
    The young flowers are blowing toward the west –
But the young, young children, O my brothers,
        They are weeping bitterly!
They are weeping in the playtime of the others,
        In the country of the free.

Do you question the young children in the sorrow
        Why their tears are falling so?
The old man may weep for his to-morrow
        Which is lost in Long Ago;
The old tree is leafless in the forest,
    The old year is ending in the frost,
The old wound, if stricken, is the sorest,
    The old hope is hardest to be lost.
But the young, young children, O my brothers,
        Do you ask them why they stand
Weeping sore before the bosoms of their mothers,
        In our happy Fatherland?

'For oh,' say the children, 'we are weary,
        And we cannot run or leap;
If we cared for any meadows, it were merely
        To drop down in them and sleep.
Our knees tremble sorely in the stooping,
    We fall upon our faces, trying to go;
And, underneath our heavy eyelids drooping,
    The reddest flower would look as pale as snow;
For, all day, we drag our burden tiring
        Through the coal-dark, underground –
Or, all day, we drive the wheels of iron
        In the factories, round and round.'

They look up with their pale and sunken faces,
        And their look is dread to see,
For they mind you of their angels in high places,
        With eyes turned on Deity! –
'How long,' they say, 'how long, O cruel nation,
    Will you stand, to move the world, on a child's
        heart, –
Stifle down with a mailed heel its palpitation,
    And tread onward to your throne amid the mart?
Our blood splashes upward, O gold-heaper,
        And your purple shows your path!
But the child's sob in the silence curses deeper
        Than the strong man in his wrath.'

That Day

I stand by the river where both of us stood,
And there is but one shadow to darken the flood;
And the path leading to it, where both used to pass,
Has the step but of one, to take dew from the grass, –
        One forlorn since that day.

The flowers of the margin are many to see;
None stoops at my bidding to pluck them for me.
The bird in the alder sings loudly and long, –
My low sound of weeping disturbs not his song,
        As thy vow did, that day.

I stand by the river, I think of the vow;
Oh, calm as the place is, vow-breaker, be thou!
I leave the flower growing, the bird unreproved;
Would I trouble *thee* rather than *them*, my belovèd, –
        And my lover that day?

Go, be sure of my love, by that treason forgiven;
Of my prayers, by the blessings they win thee from
        Heaven;
Of my grief – (guess the length of the sword by the
        sheath's)
By the silence of life, more pathetic than death's!
        Go, – be clear of that day!

Flush or Faunus

You see this dog. It was but yesterday
I mused forgetful of his presence here
Till thought on thought drew downward tear on
      tear,
When from the pillow where wet-cheeked I lay,
A head as hairy as Faunus thrust its way
Right sudden against my face, – two golden-clear
Great eyes astonished mine, – a drooping ear
Did flap me on either cheek to dry the spray!
I started first as some Arcadian
Amazed by goatly god in twilight grove,
But as the bearded vision closelier ran
My tears off, I knew Flush, and rose above
Surprise and sadness, – thanking the true PAN
Who, by low creatures, leads to heights of love.

From
A SABBATH MORNING
AT SEA

The ship went on with solemn face;
  To meet the darkness on the deep,
    The solemn ship went onward.
I bowed down weary in the place,
  For parting tears and present sleep
    Had weighed mine eyelids downward.

The new sight, the new wondrous sight!
  The waters round me, turbulent, –
    The skies impassive o'er me,
Calm, in a moonless, sunless light,
  Half glorified by that intent
    Of holding the day-glory!

Love me, sweet friends, this sabbath day!
  The sea sings round me while ye roll
    Afar the hymn unaltered,
And kneel, where once I knelt to pray,
  And bless me deeper in the soul,
    Because the voice has faltered.

And though this sabbath comes to me
   Without the stolèd minister
     Or chanting congregation,
God's spirit brings communion, HE
   Who brooded soft on waters drear,
     Creator on creation.

Himself, I think, shall draw me higher,
   Where keep the saints with harp and song
     An endless sabbath morning,
And on that sea commixed with fire
   Oft drop their eyelids, raised too long
     To the full Godhead's burning.

Hiram Powers' 'Greek Slave'

They say Ideal beauty cannot enter
The house of anguish. On the threshold stands
An alien Image with enshackled hands,
Called the Greek Slave! as if the artist meant her
(That passionless perfection which he lent her,
Shadowed not darkened where the sill expands)
To so confront man's crimes in different lands
With man's ideal sense. Pierce to the centre,
Art's fiery finger! – and break up ere long
The serfdom of this world! Appeal, fair stone,
From God's pure heights of beauty against man's
      wrong!
Catch up in thy divine face, not alone
East griefs but west, – and strike and shame the
      strong,
By thunders of white silence, overthrown.

Life

Each creature holds an insular point in space;
Yet what man stirs a finger, breathes a sound,
But all the multitudinous beings round
In all the countless worlds with time and place
For their conditions, down to the central base,
Thrill, haply, in vibration and rebound,
Life answering life across the vast profound,
In full antiphony, by a common grace?
I think this sudden joyaunce which illumes
A child's mouth sleeping, unaware may run
From some soul newly loosened from earth's tombs:
I think this passionate sigh, which half-begun
I stifle back, may reach and stir the plumes
Of God's calm angel standing in the sun.

Question and Answer

Love you seek for, presupposes
  Summer heat and sunny glow.
Tell me, do you find moss-roses
  Budding, blooming in the snow?
Snow might kill the rose-tree's root –
Shake it quickly from your foot,
  Lest it harm you as you go.

From the ivy where it dapples
  A grey ruin, stone by stone, –
Do you look for grapes and apples,
  Or for sad green leaves alone?
Pluck the leaves off, two or three –
Keep them for morality
  When you shall be safe and gone.

From
CROWNED AND BURIED

NAPOLEON! – years ago, and that great word
Compact of human breath in hate and dread
And exultation, skied us overhead –
An atmosphere whose lightning was the sword
Scathing the cedars of the world, – drawn down
In burnings, by the metal of a crown.

That name consumed the silence of the snows
In Alpine keeping, holy and cloud-hid;
The mimic eagles dared what Nature's did,
And over-rushed her moutainous repose
In search of eyries: and the Egyptian river
Mingled the same word with its grand 'For ever.'

That name was shouted near the pyramidal
Nilotic tombs, whose mummied habitants,
Packed to humanity's significance,
Motioned it back with stillness, – shouts as idle
As hireling artists' work of myrrh and spice
Which swathed last glories around the Ptolemies.

The world's face changed to hear it: kingly men
Came down in chidden babes' bewilderment
From autocratic places, each content
With sprinkled ashes for anointing: then
The people laughed or wondered for the nonce,
To see one throne a composite of thrones.

Napoleon! – 'twas a high name lifted high:
It met at last God's thunder sent to clear
Our compassing and covering atmosphere
And open a clear sight beyond the sky
Of supreme empire; this of earth's was done –
And kings crept out again to feel the sun.

From
DE PROFUNDIS

The face which, duly as the sun,
Rose up for me with life begun,
To mark all bright hours of the day
With hourly love, is dimmed away, –
And yet my days go on, go on.

The tongue which, like a stream, could run
Smooth music from the roughest stone,
And every morning with 'Good day'
Make each day good, is hushed away, –
And yet my days go on, go on.

The heart which, like a staff, was one
For mine to lean and rest upon,
The strongest on the longest day
With steadfast love, is caught away, –
And yet my days go on, go on.

The past rolls forward on the sun
And makes all night. O dreams begun,
Not to be ended! Ended bliss,
And life that will not end in this!
My days go on, my days go on.

I knock and cry, – Undone, undone!
Is there no help, no comfort, – none?
No gleaning in the wide wheat-plains
Where others drive their loaded wains?
My vacant days go on, go on.

Only to lift the turf unmown
From off the earth where it has grown,
Some cubit-space, and say 'Behold,
Creep in, poor Heart, beneath that fold,
Forgetting how the days go on.'

Take from my head the thorn-wreath brown!
No mortal grief deserves that crown.
O supreme Love, chief misery,
The sharp regalia are for THEE
Whose days eternally go on!

And having in thy life-depth thrown
Being and suffering (which are one),
As a child drops his pebble small
Down some deep well, and hears it fall
Smiling – so I. THY DAYS GO ON.

From
CASA GUIDI WINDOWS

Cimabue stood up very well
In spite of Giotto's, and Angelico
   The artist-saint kept smiling in his cell
The smile with which he welcomed the sweet slow
   Inbreak of angels (whitening through the dim
That he might paint them), while the sudden sense
   Of Raffael's future was revealed to him
By force of his own fair works' competence.
   The same blue waters where the dolphins swim
Suggest the tritons. Through the blue Immense
   Strike out, all swimmers! cling not in the way
Of one another, so to sink; but learn
   The strong man's impulse, catch the freshening
      spray
He throws up in his motions, and discern
   By his clear westering eye, the time of day.

Cold graves, we say? it shall be testified
That living men who burn in heart and brain,
  Without the dead were colder. If we tried
To sink the past beneath our feet, be sure
  The future would not stand. Precipitate
This old roof from the shrine, and, insecure,
  The nesting swallows fly off, mate from mate.
How scant the gardens, if the graves were fewer!
  The tall green poplars grew no longer straight
Whose tops not looked to Troy. Would any fight
  For Athens, and not swear by Marathon?
Who dared build temples, without tombs in sight?
  Or live, without some dead man's benison?
Or seek truth, hope for good, and strive for right,
  If, looking up, he saw not in the sun
Some angel of the martyrs all day long
  Standing and waiting? Your last rhythm will need
Your earliest key-note. Could I sing this song,
  If my dead masters had not taken heed
To help the heavens and earth to make me strong,
  As the wind ever will find out some reed
And touch it to such issues as belong
  To such a frail thing? None may grudge the Dead
Libations from full cups. Unless we choose
  To look back to the hills behind us spread,
The plains before us sadden and confuse;
  If orphaned, we are disinherited.

From
BIANCA AMONG THE NIGHTINGALES

The cypress stood up like a church
  That night we felt our love would hold,
And saintly moonlight seemed to search
  And wash the whole world clean as gold;
The olives crystallized the vales'
  Broad slopes until the hills grew strong:
The fireflies and the nightingales
  Throbbed each to either, flame and song.
The nightingales, the nightingales!

Upon the angle of its shade
  The cypress stood, self-balanced high;
Half up, half down, as double made,
  Along the ground, against the sky.
And *we* too! from such soul-height went
  Such leaps of blood, so blindly driven,
We scarce knew if our nature meant
  Most passionate earth or intense heaven.
The nightingales, the nightingales!

Giulio, my Giulio! – sing they so,
　　And you be silent? Do I speak,
And you not hear? An arm you throw
　　Round some one, and I feel so weak?
– Oh, owl-like birds! They sing for spite,
　　They sing for hate, they sing for doom!
They'll sing through death who sing through night,
　　They'll sing and stun me in the tomb –
The nightingales, the nightingales!

From
AURORA LEIGH

Aurora's Independence

With quiet indignation I broke in,
'You misconceive the question like a man,
Who sees a woman as the complement
Of his sex merely. You forget too much
That every creature, female as the male,
Stands single in responsible act and thought
As also in birth and death. Whoever says
To a loyal woman, "Love and work with me,"
Will get fair answers if the work and love,
Being good themselves, are good for her – the best
She was born for. Women of a softer mood,
Surprised by men when scarcely awake to life,
Will sometimes only hear the first word, love,
And catch up with it any kind of work,
Indifferent, so that dear love go with it.
I do not blame such women, though, for love,
They pick much oakum; earth's fanatics make
Too frequently heaven's saints. But *me* your work
Is not the best for, – nor your love the best,
Nor able to commend the kind of work
For love's sake merely.'

A Prospect of Florence

I found a house at Florence on the hill
Of Bellosguardo. 'Tis a tower which keeps
A post of double observation o'er
That valley of Arno (holding as a hand
The outspread city) straight towards Fiesole
And Mount Morello and the setting sun,
The Vallombrosan mountains opposite,
Which sunrise fills as full as crystal cups
Turned red to the brim because their wine is red.
No sun could die nor yet be born unseen
By dwellers at my villa: morn and eve
Were magnified before us in the pure
Illimitable space and pause of sky,
Intense as angels' garments blanched with God,
Less blue than radiant. From the outer wall
Of the garden, drops the mystic floating grey
Of olive trees (with interruptions green
From maise and vine), until 'tis caught and torn
Upon the abrupt black line of cypresses
Which signs the way to Florence. Beautiful
The city lies along the ample vale,
Cathedral, tower and palace, piazza and street,
The river trailing like a silver cord
Through all, and curling loosely, both before
And after, over the whole stretch of land
Sown whitely up and down its opposite slopes
With farms and villas.

SOURCES OF THE EXTRACTS

Suite of Sonnets
This selection of sonnets from the complete set, *Sonnets from the Portuguese*, has been chosen to tell the story, or, more accurately, to chart the relationship, of the poet and her lover (Elizabeth to Robert), while printing only the most attractive and accomplished works of the full complement of forty-four. The sonnets included are numbered 3, 4, 5, 10, 13, 14, 21, 26, 28, 38, 41 and 43 in the original sequence.

The Cry of the Human
Abridged from the original; stanzas 4, 5, 6, 7, 10 and 13 only are included.

The Cry of the Children
Shortened: stanzas 1, 2, 6 and 13 only are printed.

A Sabbath Morning at Sea
Shortened to include only the stanzas set by Elgar in his *Sea Pictures* – numbers 1, 3, 11, 12 and 13 of the original.

Crowned and Buried
Another long poem abridged to its essence to concentrate on the portrait of Napoleon and on his influence on dynastic Europe. Consists of stanzas 1, 4, 5, 6 and 11.

De Profundis
Stanzas 1, 2, 3, 6, 8, 12, 20 and 24 only are reproduced.

Bianca Among the Nightingales
Drastically revised to turn a discursive love poem into a lyric – stanzas 1, 2 and 16 only.

Casa Guidi Windows
First extract: Book One, lines 389–403; second extract: Book One, lines 415–41.

Aurora Leigh
First extract: Book Two, lines 434–53; second extract: Book Seven, lines 515–41.

NOTES ON THE PICTURES

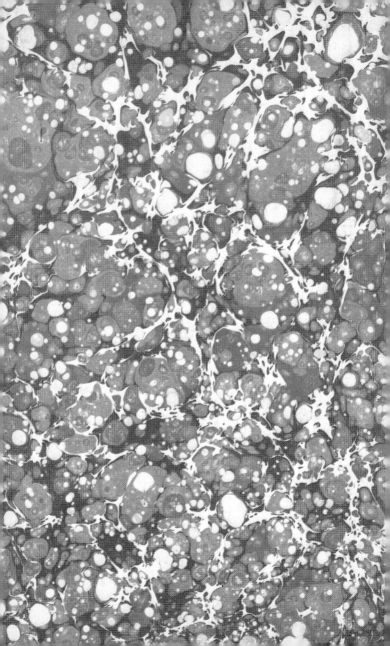